Table of Contents

Introduction

Chapter 1 Sleep Properly to Get Rid of Anxiety

Chapter 2 Herbs for Reducing Anxiety Symptoms

Chapter 3 Essential Oils

Chapter 4 Vitamins and Other Essential Nutrients

Chapter 5 Ideal Diet

Chapter 6 Beat Anxiety with Yoga

Conclusion

Text Copyright © Jeremy Messer

All rights reserved. No part of this book may be reproduced in any form without prior consent.

Legal & Disclaimer

The information contained in this book is not designed to replace or Take the place of any form of medicine or professional medical advice. The information in this book has been provided for educational and entertainment purposes only.

The information contained in this book has been collected from sources considered reliable, and it is accurate to the best of the Author's knowledge. The Author cannot guarantee its accuracy and validity and cannot be held liable for any errors or omissions. Updates are periodically made to this book. Please consult your doctor about the use of the natural remedies that are mentioned in this book.

Introduction

Are you suffering from a severe anxiety disorder or having panic attacks at regular intervals? If yes, this book will be your best friend. You will find this book useful even if you want to prevent yourself from falling prey to anxiety disorder.

Anxiety is the most common mental illness in America. They are over 40 million adults battling with this disorder according to the Anxiety and Depression Association of America. More than one in 10 Americans have prescribed medication for this disorder.

While these drugs help us in coping with the symptoms of anxiety, they also expose us to a series of debilitating side effects. Natural remedies for anxiety, on the other hand, ensure that we can get rid of the problem seamlessly without suffering from any adverse effect.

If you're looking for an instant cure you will not find it here. Beating anxiety is a process and a process takes time. Using these natural remedies you find in this book will help you WIN the battle with anxiety.

Chapter 1

Sleep Properly to Get Rid of Anxiety

Studies have shown that a large number of people become victims of anxiety due to lack of proper sleep. In addition, eight hours of sound sleep on a daily basis has been proven to be one of the strongest remedies of this disorder. Here are some tips that will allow you to sleep better.

Ban the blue light

Psychologists suggest that the light emitted by energy-efficient light bulbs and electronics, which is commonly referred to as the blue light, has an extremely powerful effect on the master clock in our body. At night, this light prevents us from winding down our senses and thereby stops us from falling asleep. So, to have a good night's sleep, one should turn off his/her phone, tablet, television set etc. a minimum of one hour before going to bed. Dimming the lights in the bedroom is also a must.

Don't take naps

I know that due to hectic work schedule often it becomes difficult for you to spend an entire day without taking naps. However, if you want to sleep well at night, you will have to stop taking those naps. If you struggle to eliminate them completely from your daily schedule, make sure they are not more than 20 minutes long.

Don't remain stuck in your bed when finding it hard to fall asleep

If you fail to fall asleep even after being in bed for 20 minutes, I would suggest you get up and start doing something relaxing. You can cut vegetables for the next day, read a book or even go to your garden for a relaxing walk. If you stay in your bed and keep turning and tossing, you would actually be signaling your brain to not fall asleep.

Maintain a fixed wake-up time

It's difficult to have control on the time when we fall asleep, but we can always decide the time when we would like to start our day. If we wake up every day at the same time, it will eventually fix our sleep routine and make falling asleep much easier.

Adopt good habits

Adopting the following habits can help you to fall asleep promptly:

- Eliminate noise from your bedroom. White-noise machines can help you to block sounds and have a disturbance-free sleep.

- Stay away from soda, coffee, and other caffeine-rich items. You should never consume them at night.

- Keep the temperature of your bedroom between 67 and 68 degrees Fahrenheit.

- Exercise regularly.

Chapter 2

Herbs for Reducing Anxiety Symptoms

You may be suffering from anxiety symptoms due to a recent event or might have had the problem for a long time there are certain herbs that can make the situation better for you. If used regularly and in right proportions, these herbs can also eliminate your anxiety symptoms permanently. Read on to know about some herbs you can use for fighting anxiety effectively.

Ginger root

The active ingredients present in ginger root make it a highly effective remedy for anxiety. You can consume ginger extracts in form of capsules or can inhale ginger oil to alleviate symptoms of anxiety. Consuming 2 to 4 grams (pregnant women, however, shouldn't consume more than 1 gram of ginger extract) of ginger extracts every day should be enough to relieve the symptoms. Avoid this herbal remedy if you have been diagnosed with a bleeding disorder or take a blood-thinning drug.

If you want to offer protection to your family against stress and angst, add ginger root to marinades, stir-fries, and salads.

Valerian

Studies conducted for finding out the medicinal benefits of valerian have revealed that the herb is instrumental in managing nervous restlessness, insomnia, and anxiety. This herb is available at powder, tincture, tea and fluid extracts at the health food stores and pharmacies.

Take a cupful of valerian tea 1 to 2 hours before going to bed. To prepare the tea, put 1 teaspoon of dried root of valerian in a cup of boiling hot water for 5 minutes. Having this tea before bedtime will promote sound sleep and thereby reduce your anxiety symptoms. This herb has been found to show amazing results even when consumed in cognition with other calming herbs like lemon balm and passion flower.

You should never take valerian before operating heavy pieces of machinery and during the daytime. Use of this herb should also be avoided prior to surgeries or when treated with medicinal drugs like statins, antihistamines, and sedatives.

Passionflower

This herb works by promoting better sleep and offering a sense of calm. Herbalists often prescribe passionflower for treating insomnia triggered by anxiety. The herb can also help people experiencing anxious flutters in their stomach. Pregnant women, however, should stay away from passion flower as its active ingredients are known for contracting the uterus.

Chamomile

Chamomile has been used for fighting stress, insomnia, and anxiety since ancient times. Findings of modern-day scientific research also suggest that the herb is highly beneficial for combating mild to moderate anxiety disorder. For best results, you must consume this herb in form of herbal tea. For preparing the tea, put 2-3 teaspoons of dried chamomile flower in a cupful of boiling hot water. Allow the herb to soak for around 15 minutes, sift and drink it slowly. For best results, have this tea two to three times every day and don't forget to have it before going to bed.

You should avoid using this herbal remedy if you are taking blood-thinners, sedatives, statins, or contraceptive pills.

Lemon balm

Lemon balm helps in relieving two of the most common symptoms of anxiety, difficulty in falling asleep and decreased appetite. You can use it in combination with chamomile and valerian for increasing its ability to promote relaxation. Lemon balm is rich in phytochemicals like tannins and eugenol. These active ingredients of the herb provide it with the ability to fight bacteria, fungus, and viruses. Terpene, a substance found in the essential oil extracted from the leaves of lemon balm plant, on the other hand, is known for promoting relaxation.

People suffering from anxiety should take this herb in form of capsules. Taking 300-500 mg of the herb two to three times daily is usually enough to eradicate the symptoms of anxiety.

Nursing moms and pregnant women should consult their physicians before using lemon balm.

St John's wort

This herb is used widely for treating mild-moderate depression and anxiety. St. John's Wort is sold in form of liquid extracts, commercial tea, tablets, and capsules. Take 300 mg of the herb thrice daily. Soon, you'll find that all your anxiety symptoms are gone. Never consume this herb if you are taking contraceptive pills, allergy drugs, sedatives or antidepressants. It's also not meant for breastfeeding or pregnant women.

Chapter 3

Essential Oils

Lavender

Lavender is known for its pleasant smell and calming effects. It is used widely for inducing relaxation and relieving stress. It's considered a nervous system restorative and helps with inner peace, sleep, restlessness, irritability and panic attacks. Remember, boys who are yet to attain puberty should never consume or inhale lavender.

Below, I have listed a few methods of using lavender for fighting anxiety and stress.

- Take 2-3 cups boiling hot water and add 2-4 drops lavender essential oil to it. Inhale the vapor for a few minutes and see all your anxiety symptoms vanishing almost instantly.

- Before getting in the bed at night, take a bottle of lavender spray and use three to four squirts on your pillow and bedding.

- Take 3 drops of pure lavender oil, and 1 teaspoon of fractionated coconut or almond oil, blend them in your hand and then rub onto your neck.

Rose

It's perhaps the second most common essential oil to help alleviate anxiety behind lavender. The smell of a rose is one of those experiences that instantly bring a smile to your face because of its beautiful smell. When you're getting ready for bed place five drops in a diffuser by your nightstand.

Hopefully, when you awake you will feel refreshed and at peace.

Vetiver

It has been used for its ability to help control and reduce anxiety, emotions, such as heart rate, blood pressure, and respiration. It is believed that Vetiver has a similar impact as Diazepam, which is a medication that treats anxiety.

- Put 5-10 drops of Vetiver oil in your bath water, it's both fragrant and cooling, using it in your bath prevents overheating and helps with relaxation and insomnia. To boost the calming results, combine vetiver oil with lavender and rose essential oils as well.
- Diffusing 3-5 drops of vetiver oil or place 1-2 drops on your wrist, chest, and neck, it will help benefit your mind and mood.
- Make your own calming massage oil by mixing 3-5 drops of vetiver oil with equal parts of jojoba oil. This combination will leave your skin feeling clean and moisturized and your mind at peace.

Ylang Ylang

Ylang Ylang helps treat anxiety due to its calming and uplifting effects. It gives your courage, optimism and helps ease fearfulness. It is considered a moderately strong sedative which can calm heart agitation and nervous palpitations. This oil can be diffused throughout your home with the use of a diffuser or inhaled directly from the bottle. Yland Ylang can also be applied topically. It should be diluted with coconut oil in a 1:1 ratio before applying it to your skin. Please keep it away from your eyes, ears or nose.

Do not use Ylang Ylang if you have low blood pressure.

Bergamot

Bergamot is a plant that produces a type of citrus fruit, it's classified as a hybrid between a sour orange and lemon. The peel of the fruit is where the oil is taken from and they use it to make medicine. Bergamot oil is a relaxant it reduces nervous tension and feelings of stress and anxiety. This powerful oil can stimulate hormones, such as dopamine and serotonin, which create feelings of sedation and relaxation. Relieve stress and anxiety by using bergamot oil in a diffuser or oil burner.

The smell of oil leads to a feeling of ease and contentment.

- Use bergamot oil by rubbing 2-3 drops into your hand and cupping your mouth and nose. Breathe in the oil slowly. Try rubbing the oil on your feet and stomach as well.
- Bergamot oil can also be used in a diffuser or oil burner to help alleviate anxiety.

Frankincense

Frankincense can help reduce pain, inflammation, chronic stress, and anxiety. It is used by inhaling the oil for absorbing it the skin usually mixed with a carrier oil, such as jojoba oil. It's believed that the oil transmits messages to the limbic system of the brain, which is known to influence the nervous system. To fight anxiety place 3-5 drops of this oil in a diffuser or a vaporizer. Frankincense can also be added to a warm bath to induce a feeling of relaxation and peace.

Please do not ingest large quantities as it can be toxic.

Chapter 4

Vitamins and Other Essential Nutrients

There are certain essential nutrients that will allow you to fight anxiety more effectively. Read through the section below to get acquainted with them.

Vitamin B complex

The majority of us know that B vitamins play extremely essential roles in allowing our brain to function properly. So, it shouldn't surprise you that being deficient of these vitamins can result in anxiety and depression, disorders triggered by an imbalance of chemicals in our brain. Some of the common symptoms of vitamin B deficiency include headaches, nervousness, fatigue, rapid heartbeat etc. If you are experiencing these symptoms, you should undergo blood tests to find out whether you are deficient of vitamin B. The best way of getting rid of the problem quickly is taking 100% natural supplements of the vitamins. In addition, you should also include food items rich in the nutrients in your daily diet.

Magnesium

Nutritionists often describe magnesium as the mood-stabilizing mineral. If you are suffering from magnesium deficiency you are surely at higher risk of developing anxiety. Supplementation of the mineral will not only relax your mind but will also alleviate other anxiety symptoms such as insomnia, anxiousness and muscle tremors.

Magnesium is one of the main constituents of chlorophyll, the agent responsible for giving leafy greens and green vegetables their color. So, a great way of getting rid of magnesium deficiency is including more and more green vegetables and leafy greens in your daily diet. If your diet consists of a lot of these magnesium-rich food items, take 300 grams of magnesium supplement per day. Increase the amount to 500 grams if you fail to include enough greens in your daily diet.

Omega 3 fatty acids

Several studies have confirmed that there's an association between, omega 3 fatty acids and our mood. This essential nutrient plays a significant role in stabilizing our mood when we suffer from excessive stress. The type of omega 3 fatty acid used for managing anxiety is EPA or eicosapentaenoic acid. It is one of the main active ingredients of fish oil capsules and is often described as a powerful nutrient for the mind. According to nutritionists, consumption of 1.5 g to 4 g of EPA is enough for improving and stabilizing mood of people suffering from anxiety disorder. Other than having omega 3 fatty acid supplements, you should also eat fish a minimum of three times every week.

Vitamin D

Lack of sun exposure is known for causing an emotional disorder called SAD (seasonal affective disorder). This disorder is actually a result of vitamin D deficiency and is marked by severe depression and anxiety symptoms. Supplementation of vitamin D3 has been found to be effective for patients suffering from SAD. People living in cold regions that seldom get sunlit days are the ones at maximum risk of developing this condition. A great way of preventing an occurrence of SAD is consumption of 1000 mg vitamin D3 every day, especially during the winter months.

Vitamin C

According to the findings of a recent study, as much as 70% of people suffering from anxiety and other mental health issues were found to have scurvy, a condition resulting from vitamin C deficiency. In addition, researchers have also found that being deficient of vitamin C reduces our ability to deal with stress and causes a significant reduction in the development of neurotransmitters having links with anxiety. So, people suffering from anxiety should ensure that they are having vitamin C in the right quantities. Try to consume 1000-2000 mg of the vitamin per day in form of supplements as well as food items like citrus fruits.

Chapter 5

Ideal Diet for People with Anxiety

If you want to get rid of your anxiety symptoms, you should consider making some changes in your daily diet. The section below will tell you what you should eat and what you shouldn't to lead a stress-free life.

Food items you must avoid when fighting anxiety

1. **Caffeine-rich food items-** There are many people who cannot do without their morning coffee. If you have any such habit and you are trying to get rid of anxiety, tell yourself that you should stop loving your morning coffee as soon as possible. I am not telling you just to stay away from coffee. Coffee is just one of the many caffeine-rich food items that can have a strong negative impact on your mood. Some other examples of such items include tea, energy drinks, etc.

   Excessive consumption of caffeine can make you victims of side effects like sleeping disorders, rapid heartbeat, seizure etc. If you continue having caffeine-rich food products in spite of experiencing the above symptoms, you will eventually develop a severe anxiety disorder.

2. **Food items containing additives-** Manmade food additives are used frequently for adding fresh flavor and enhancing the appearance of different food items we consume. This is done in spite of the fact that the majority of these additives are harmful to our physical and emotional health. Below I have listed some widely used food additives that can trigger anxiety.

   - **Aspartame-** Aspartame or Sweetener (951) is used as a sugar substitute in a range of products, which include sugar-free gums, soft drinks, and some tabletop sweeteners. Several studies conducted in recent times have found links between regular intakes of this addictive with anxiety.

   - **HFSC-** HFCS or high fructose corn syrup is a common ingredient found in many processed foods. This additive has been found to cause a range of health disorders including anxiety.

- **MSG-** MSG or monosodium glutamate is categorized as an amino acid. It is primarily used for adding flavors to snacks, frozen foods, dressings, and soups. Being an excitotoxin, MSG leaves our brain cells highly excited. Overconsumption of this food addictive might even damage our brain cells permanently. Studies have shown that consuming MSG regularly can make people suffer from anxiety symptoms such as fatigue and headaches.

- **Food dyes-** Yellow #5 and Red #40, two of the most widely used food dyes, have been found to disrupt the functioning of our nervous system and increase anxiety symptoms.

3. **Salt-** Food items containing an excessive amount of salt increases our blood pressure and forces our heart to work much harder. This leads to secretion of the stress hormone

called adrenaline and invites tension and edginess. So, if you are suffering from anxiety, you should eliminate all salty foods from your diet. Normal people, on the other hand, should avoid consuming salty foods before bedtime as they might stop them from falling asleep easily by triggering stress and restlessness.

If you want to keep anxiety symptoms at bay, stay away from fast foods and processed foods as these are the items that often contain an excessive amount of salt. You must also be careful when cooking at home. If you have anxiety, replace salt with spices and herbs for making your food tasty.

4. **Sugar-** Food items containing refined sugars are your biggest enemies if you have anxiety. When we consume sugar we experience a temporary burst of energy, which is followed by a drop in the blood sugar levels. This makes us fatigued and lethargic. In addition, one may also start feeling anxious. When our blood sugar levels fluctuate constantly, our body starts releasing cortisol and adrenalin, agents

known for triggering panic attacks and anxiety symptoms.

5. **Alcohol-** Alcohol plays the role of a depressant and prevents secretion of serotonin, a mood-regulating neurotransmitter. In addition, alcohol hinders our metabolism significantly. One should never have alcohol at night as by altering our blood sugar and hydration levels, alcohol can stop us from having a restful sleep.

The food you must eat when fighting anxiety

1. **Fish-** Fish is a rich source of B vitamins and proteins, nutrients that work by taming tension. In addition, it also contains high levels of omega 3 fatty acids, nutrients known for reducing cardiovascular diseases, controlling blood sugar levels and fueling neurons responsible for treating and preventing anxiety and depression. Another major anti-anxiety nutrient you can get from fish is magnesium, a mineral that promotes relaxation by soothing our nerves.

2. **Asparagus-** It is a rich source of folate, a B vitamin responsible for converting folic acid

in our body. Several studies conducted to date have linked anxiety and depression with folic acid deficiency. As a result, most nutritionists recommend asparagus to patients suffering from anxiety symptoms.

3. **Greek yogurt-** You should consume the unsweetened and plain version of Greek yogurt for maximum benefits. Every 6 ounce of this fat-free yogurt contains nearly 22 g protein but makes you consume just 120 calories. Greek yogurt alleviates anxiety symptoms by reducing blood pressure. In addition, it is a rich source of Vitamin B12 and B6, both of which are known to play vital roles in regulating our brain functions.

4. **Almonds-** The primary nutrients present in almonds are manganese, magnesium, potassium, plant protein, healthy fats, and vitamin E. Their slight sweetness and crunch make them extremely satisfying and decrease your chances of engaging in binge-eating. For enjoying these benefits, you should choose a handful of raw almonds instead of the packages that contain salted varieties.

5. **Spinach-** The high magnesium content of this veggie makes them a must have for every

individual suffering from anxiety. Just having a cup of spinach will fill 40% of your daily quota of this miracle mineral. In addition, a cup of spinach also contains 5 grams protein. This veggie is also a rich source of folate.

6. **Oats-** Oats contain a high level of fiber, magnesium and B vitamins. All these nutrients are vital for alleviating anxiety. In addition, oats also promote the production of serotonin, the brain chemical known for its antidepressant effects. I would suggest you go for whole oats instead of the instant varieties. It's because the instant ones often contain an excessive amount of refined sugar or artificial sweeteners.

Chapter 6

Beat Anxiety with Yoga

Any kind of physical activity is good for people suffering from anxiety symptoms or those looking for preventing anxiety disorder. One can go for walks, jog, swim, or join aerobic classes to get rid of anxiety. However, the form of exercise that is known to offer maximum benefits to people with anxiety is yoga asana.

I would, however, suggest you practice all the three forms of yoga, pranayama or breathing exercises, dhyana or meditation, and asana or free hand exercises.

Pranayama will help you in freeing your mind by eliminating all the unnecessary thoughts and beliefs accumulated in it. Meditation or dhyana will assist you in relaxing your distracted mind, provide you with a sense of peace and calm and ensure that your mind functions properly all through the day. You must practice pranayama and dhyana every day. Pranayama should ideally be practiced early in the morning in an empty stomach and meditation should be practiced every night before going to bed.

Yoga postures you should perform for beating anxiety

Child's pose

Yoga experts usually refer to child's pose as a position of rest. Usually, people use it for regrouping or relaxing in between tougher and more challenging yoga postures. However, this posture has some serious benefits for people suffering from anxiety. Child's pose assists in releasing tension from our shoulders, neck, and back, which are body parts holding the maximum amount of stress. In addition, the pose is also known for promoting relaxation by enabling steady and conscious breathing. Below are the steps of performing this asana.

1) Sit on the heels. You can sit directly on the floor if you want or can lay a yoga mat and sit on it.

2) Depending on what appears more comfortable for you, you can keep the knees apart or together.

3) Lower your forehead and bend forward slowly until your forehead touches the floor. Exhale as you do this.

4) Your arms should be beside your body and your palms should face the ceiling.

5) Start pressing your chest gently onto your thighs. If your knees are kept apart, you should press your chest in between your thighs.

6) Stay in this position for 45 to 60 seconds. Initially, you may struggle to be in this position for such a long time. So, you can start with 15 seconds and then increase the duration gradually.

7) You should pay significant attention to your breathing when performing the child's pose. When inhaling, imagine that you are breathing from the navel pulling it towards the spine. When exhaling relax your arms and body. Repeat 4 to 12 times.

8) Now, put your palms beneath your shoulders and raise the upper body slowly. Stop after reaching your initial sitting position. You should inhale while doing this.

9) Relax.

Viparita Karani or the legs up the wall pose

This yoga pose is taught in every restorative yoga class. This shows how beneficial it is for enabling restoration. Other than reducing anxiety symptoms, this pose is also great at alleviating lower back pain. You will also get rid of anxiety symptoms like high blood pressure and insomnia if you perform this asana regularly. You can perform this pose in every single place that has a wall. However, I would suggest you perform it only in places that are comfortable to you and are serene.

Yoga therapists talk about two different ways of practicing the legs up the wall pose, as a supported position, which would require you to use props, and as an unsupported position without using any prop. Both these options would provide you with similar benefits. However, some people find the first version more relaxing than the second. You will need a sturdy door or a wall on which you will be able to place your legs when performing both the versions. Here are the steps of the legs up the wall pose:

1. If you are performing the supported pose, place a long, firm pillow or a bolster against the wall.

2. Sit with the left side of your body against the wall. You should have the lower back resting on the pillow if you are performing the supported pose.

3. Now, turn to the left and slowly slide the legs up the wall. Those who are using a pillow will have to shift their back onto it before sliding the legs up. Using your

hands is a must for maintaining balance when shifting body weight.

4. Lower the back onto the pillow/floor and relax. Your head and shoulders should be rested on the ground.

5. Scoot the buttocks against the wall while shifting your body weight from one side to another. Your arms should be kept on your sides with the palms facing the ceiling. At this point, individuals using a pillow should have their lower back supported fully by the prop.

6. Release the tension from the thigh bones and relax.

7. Hold this position for 5 minutes (you can increase the duration up to 10 minutes once you become a veteran at performing this asana). Make sure you have your eyes closed. Also, don't forget to focus on your breathing.

8. When releasing, push your body away from the wall as slowly as possible. Then, gently slide down the legs to your right.

Allow your body to come back to a sitting position using your hands.

Vriksasana or the tree-pose

This is possibly the yoga asana used most frequently by people experiencing anxiety symptoms. Practicing this pose will allow you to promote awareness and increase your ability to concentrate. This will help you to distract your mind from all the anxious thoughts and focus more on positive things in life. The best thing about this pose is that you will need minimum space for performing it. You can perform it whenever you need to relax and have some time in hand. Find out how to perform the tree-pose.

1. Stand with your back straight. Your feet should be together.

2. Slowly fold your right leg and move it upwards to place it on the top portion of your left thigh. The toes of your right leg must point downwards. In addition, your right leg should form an angle of 90 degrees with your left leg.

3. Now, slowly extend both your arms over the head.

4. Take a deep breath and allow the palms of your two hands to meet over your head.

5. Stay in this pose for 30 seconds. Gradually increase your time. You can stay in this position as long as you want. Your balance should be perfect as for experiencing the benefits of the tree pose having proper balance is a must.

6. When releasing, exhale deeply and slowly bring the arms down. Finally, bring your leg down.

7. Repeat all the above steps with your left leg. This would complete a single round of the tree pose.

8. For maximum benefits perform 4 to 5 rounds.

Salamba Sirsasana or the supported headstand

If you are anxious, you should practice the supported headstand. This yoga pose will not only help you to get rid of anxious thoughts but will also improve your chronic anxiety symptoms quickly and effectively. This position works by reversing the flow of blood in our body, which makes us focus more on our breath. Eventually, we start forgetting our discomforts and anxieties. People who perform supported headstand regularly experience contentment and calmness.

The supported headstand pose increases the flow of blood to the head. This change enables detoxification of the adrenal gland, which effectively reduces depression symptoms. Find out how to perform this amazing yoga pose.

1. You will have to use a yoga mat or a blanket when performing this yoga pose; never perform it on a bare floor as that might invite head injury.

2. Spread the blanket or yoga mat against a wall. Pile a couple of stacks, each with three yoga blocks, against the same wall. The distance between the two piles must be a little more than your head's width.

3. Stand to face the wall and kneel. Keep the hands on the floor just in front of the yoga blocks. Your fingertips should touch the blocks. Now, slowly place the shoulders on them. Your head should be pointed towards the floor.

4. Stretch the legs with care and slide both your feet together towards your hands.

5. Now, bend in any one of your knees so that the heel can come close to the butt. Once you are comfortable with the position, bend in the other knee and bring the heel near the butt. Inhale deeply and move to the next step.

6. Start stretching your legs as if you are trying to touch the ceiling with them. Allow your feet to relax against the wall. Take a minimum of three deep breaths. That's it. You are done.

7. You should be extremely careful when releasing this position.

Conclusion

In this book, I have presented a series of natural remedies for anxiety for you. I am confident these tips and tools can decrease and even eliminate the toughest of anxiety disorders. Please consult your physician if your anxiety continues or increases dramatically.

www.ingramcontent.com/pod-product-compliance
Lightning Source LLC
Chambersburg PA
CBHW051136250726
48655CB00007B/3087